To:

From:

Smitten with KITTENS

MUSINGS FROM THE LITTERBOX OF LIFE

Written & compiled by KIT E. McWHISKERS

As meowed & caterwauled to

MARA CONLON

PETER PAUPER PRESS, INC.

WHITE PLAINS, NEW YORK

For my kitty litter of friends
—M.C.

Designed by Taryn R. Sefecka

See page 81 for photo credits.

Peter Pauper Press, Inc.
202 Mamaroneck Avenue
White Plains, NY 10601

ISBN 978-1-59359-910-2
Printed in China
7 6 5

Smitten with KITTENS

MUSINGS FROM THE LITTERBOX OF LIFE

INTRODUCTION

As Cleocatra once purred, "Be it known that we, the greatest, are misunderstood." Some humans (particularly those with dogs) think that we kitties have a cattitude problem. They think we strut around like we own the world, like everything revolves around us, and that we firmly believe that all those sun-spilled nooks, crooks, and crannies are indeed specifically made for us to snooze in. (Well, aren't they?)

All right, to be purrfectly honest with you—we do think pretty highly of ourselves. But hey, what's not to love? As a class, we are a talented litter. Which is why I have scratched this book to showcase some of us and our cat legends—composers, world leaders, philosophers, authors, actors, playwrights, and musicians—who over the years have somehow had their words misattributed, or in even some cases, outright stolen! (My editor also insisted on including some expressions from humans cool enough to be considered honorary cats.)

My furrvent wish is that you curl up with your favorite feline and enjoy this little collection—fresh from the litterbox of life.

—*Kit*

EVERYBODY LIKES
A COMPLIMENT—
CATS, HOWEVER,
DEMAND THEM.

Abracat Lincoln

I'm
waiting.

Lettin' the cat outta the bag is a whole lot easier 'n puttin' it back in.

WILL ROGERS

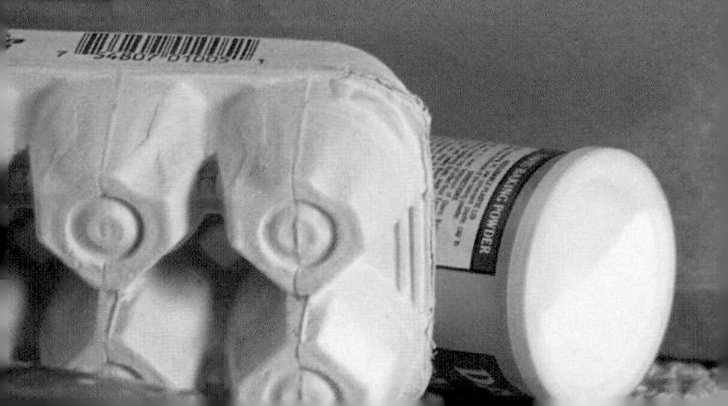

I tried being reasonable. I didn't like it.

CLINT EASTWOOD

Keep your eyes
on the stars,
and your claws
in the couch.

Tabby Roosevelt

ALL THE WORLD'S A STAGE, AND ALL THE CATS AND KITTENS MERELY PLAYERS.

William Shakespaw

Pour the milk, and they

will come. –*Saucer of Dreams*

And why should we?

Cats, as a class,
have never completely
got over the snootiness
caused by the fact that in
Ancient Egypt they
were worshiped as gods.

P. G. WODEHOUSE

I usually take a two hour nap from one to four.

YOGI BERRA

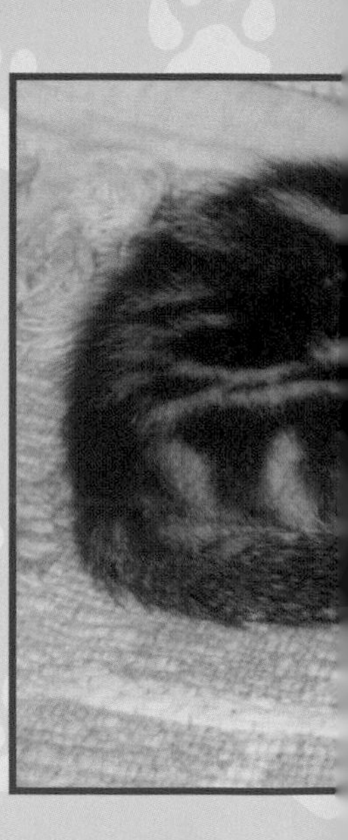

A DAY WITHOUT LAUGHTER IS A DAY WASTED.

Charlie Chaplin

Cats do not go
for a walk
to get somewhere
but to explore.

SIDNEY DENHAM

CATS SEEM TO GO
ON THE PRINCIPLE
THAT IT NEVER
DOES ANY HARM
TO ASK FOR
WHAT YOU WANT.

Joseph Wood Krutch

Winning isn't everything, it's the only thing.

VINCE LOMBARDI

To err is feline—
but it feels divine.

MEOW WEST

The answer
my feline,
is purrin' in
the wind,
The answer
is purrin' in
the wind.

CAT DYLAN

DOGS HAVE OWNERS, CATS HAVE STAFF.

Author unknown

O what a tangled web of yarn we weave, Once our owners up and leave.

SIR WHISKERS SCOTT

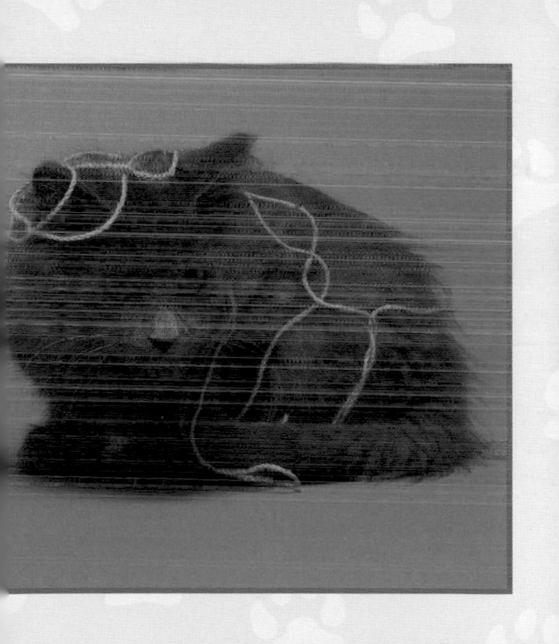

Everykitty dance now!

Of all the kitty litter joints in all the towns in all the world, she walks into mine.

HUMPHREY BOCAT

Fluffiness is overrated, anyway.

I'm good enough,
I'm smart enough,
and doggone it,
people like me.

STUART SMALLEY

Now, as you all know, there is nothing a cat dislikes so much as water; just watch your kitty shake her paws daintily when she steps into a puddle, and see how disgusted she is if a drop of water falls on her nose and back.

Agnes A. Sandham

Cats never strike a pose that isn't photogenic.

Lilian Jackson Braun

Don't hate me because
I'm beautiful.

Steppin' out with
my kitty,
Fur will fly, she's
outta sight.
It's for meow,
not for maybe,
We be struttin'
out tonight!

Irving Purrlin

No, really. I'm fine. I just need a minute to collect myself.

The cat is, above all things, a dramatist.

MARGARET BENSON

As God is my witness, I'll never eat dry cat food again!

CATLETT O'HARA

Really, what's not to love?

I don't know why we're here, but I'm pretty sure it's in order to sleep, stretch, and sleep some more.

LUDWIG KITTYGENSTEIN, PHILOSOPHER

Arrr Matey!

ME THINKS YOU BEST BE WALKIN' THE PLANK WITH THAT THERE DRY FOOD, AND SERVIN' ME SOME FRESH FISH!

BLACKBEARD KITTY

The un-leisurely life is not worth living.

SOCATES

That's one small
step for cat,
one giant leap
for catkind.

NEIL PAWSTRONG

YOU ARE ONLY YOUNG
ONCE, BUT YOU CAN BE
IMMATURE FOR A LIFETIME.

JOHN P. GRIER

Two roads diverged near the pet store, And I—I took the one that smelled of catnip and fish, And I've been a well-filled feline ever since.

CLAWBERT FROST

So many naps to take, so little time.

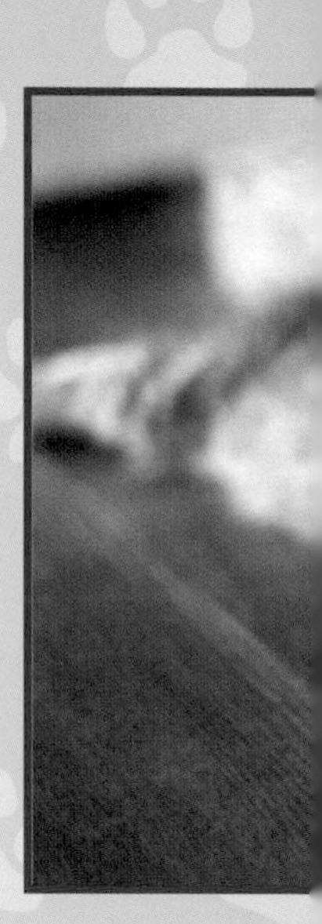

Wait!

DON'T ANYBODY MOVE!

I DROPPED MY

CONTACT LENS.

A cat must have a sunny window and a room of her own if she is to live comfortably.

PURRGINIA WOOLF

I CAN'T BELIEVE
I'VE BEEN WALKING
AROUND ALL DAY
WITH TUNA STUCK
IN MY TEETH—AND
NOBODY TOLD ME!

Home is where
the kitty is.

Good cat owners aren't born, they are made.

VINCE LOMPAWDI

Every dog must have his day—
but every day is cat day!

JOHNNY CAT SWIFT

PHOTO CREDITS

Cover & Pages 1 & 3: © GK Hart/Vikki Hart/
The Image Bank/Getty Images

Pages 5, 7, 16-17, 23, 24-25, 26, 28-29, 30,
42, 47, 48-49, 52-53, 66, 80:
© Media Bakery/Digital Vision

Pages 8-9, 36-37, 50, 64-65:
© JupiterImages/Comstock.com

Page 10: © Photo 24/Brand X Pictures

Pages 12-13, 71, 79: © Media Bakery/Corbis

Page 15: © Corbis

Pages 18, 40-41, 56-57, 59, 63:
© Media Bakery/Brand X Pictures

Pages 20-21: © Richard Sefecka

Pages 31, 32-33, 34, 44-45, 54, 68-69,
72-73, 76-77: © Media Bakery/Photodisc

Page 60-61: © Media Bakery/Thinkstock

Page 74: © Media Bakery/Stockbyte